KENNY CHESNEY
GREATEST HITS II

ISBN 978-1-4234-8467-7

HAL•LEONARD®
CORPORATION
7777 W. BLUEMOUND RD. P.O. BOX 13819 MILWAUKEE, WI 53213

Visit Hal Leonard Online at
www.halleonard.com

OUT LAST NIGHT

Words and Music by KENNY CHESNEY
and BRETT JAMES

must have — sur - vived, — and that I lived — to

go out with — my friends a - gain — to - night. — Oh, — we went —

D.S. al Coda

CODA

Repeat and Fade

Optional Ending

LIVING IN FAST FORWARD

Words and Music by DAVID LEE MURPHY
and RIVERS RUTHERFORD

The

slow. Yeah, I need to re-wind real slow. Yeah, I

still got some miles to go.

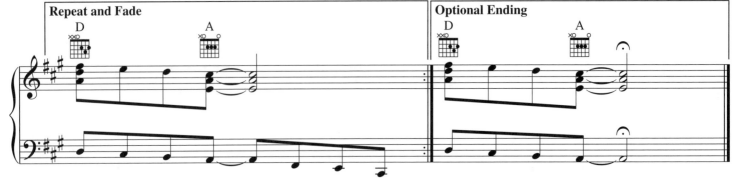

Repeat and Fade

Optional Ending

YOUNG

Words and Music by CRAIG WISEMAN,
NAOISE SHERIDAN and STEVE McEWAN

SUMMERTIME

Words and Music by STEVE McEWAN
and CRAIG WISEMAN

DOWN THE ROAD

Written by MAC McANALLY

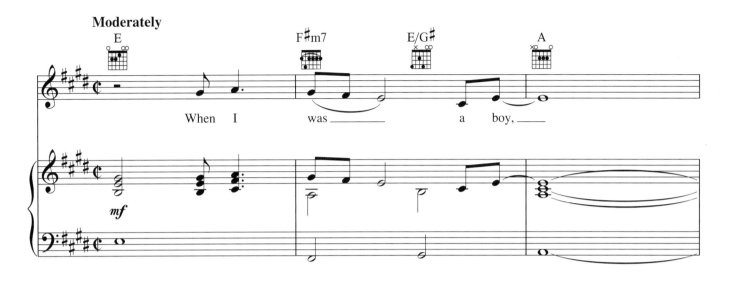

Moderately

When I was _____ a boy, _____

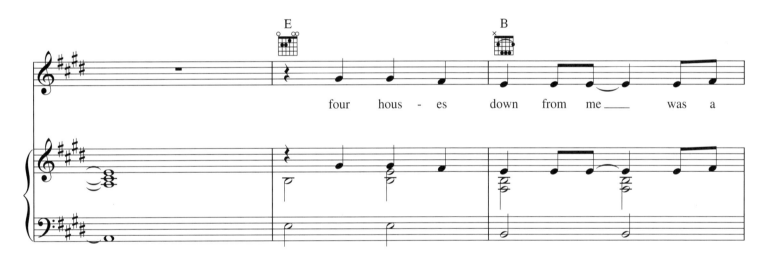

four hous - es down from me _____ was a

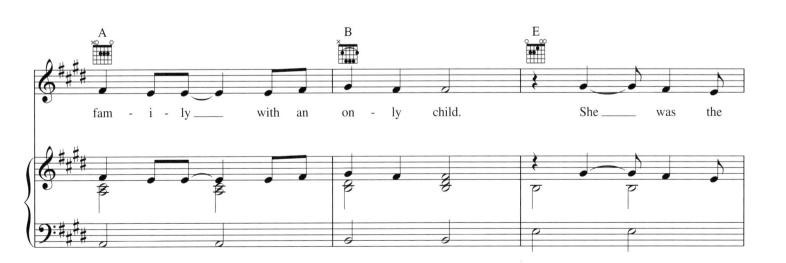

fam - i - ly _____ with an on - ly child. She _____ was the

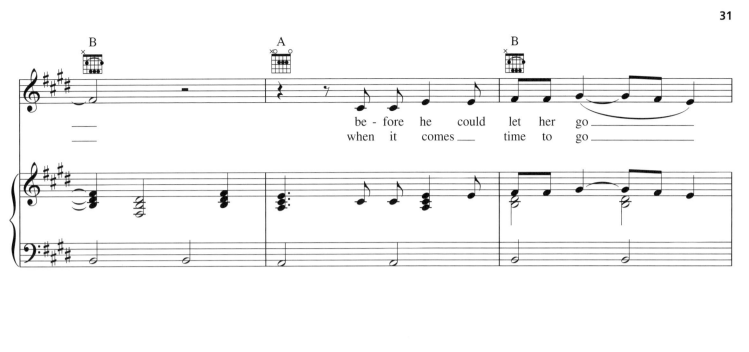

be - fore he could let her go ___
when it comes ___ time to go ___

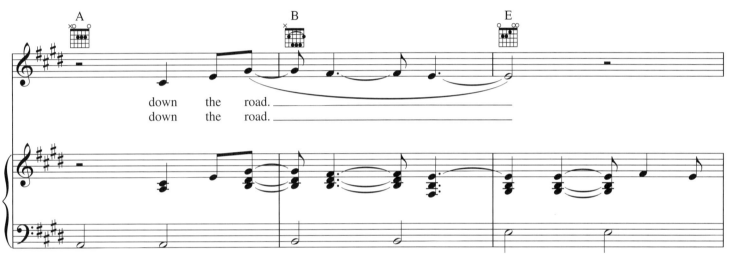

down the road. ___
down the road. ___

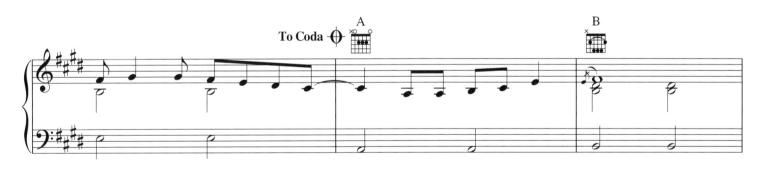

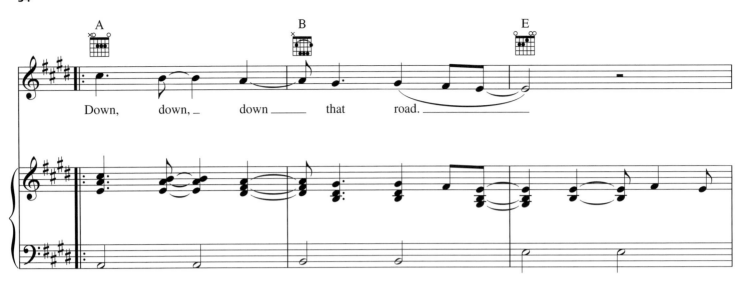

Down, down, down that road.

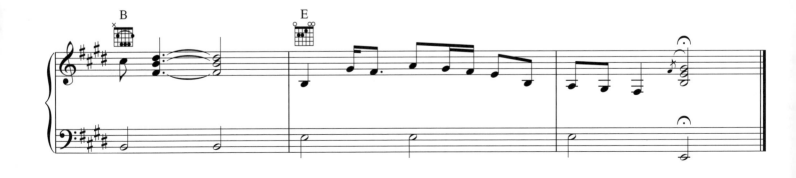

BEER IN MEXICO

Words and Music by
KENNY CHESNEY

Moderately fast

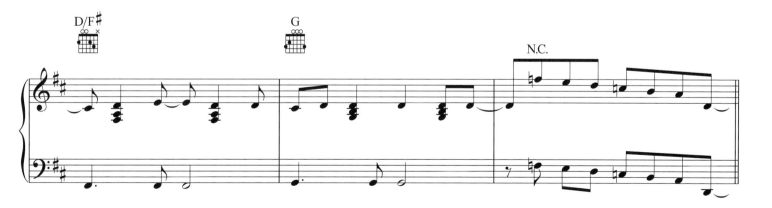

May - be I'll   set - tle down,

down _ in Mex - i - co. _____

Repeat and Fade

Optional Ending

THERE GOES MY LIFE

Words and Music by NEIL THRASHER
and WENDELL MOBLEY

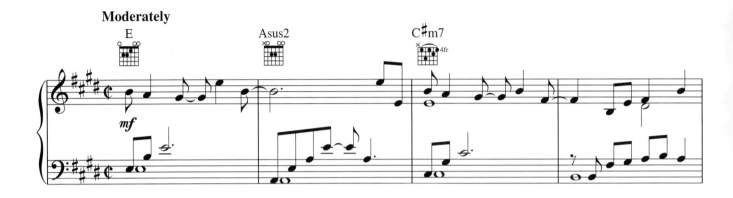

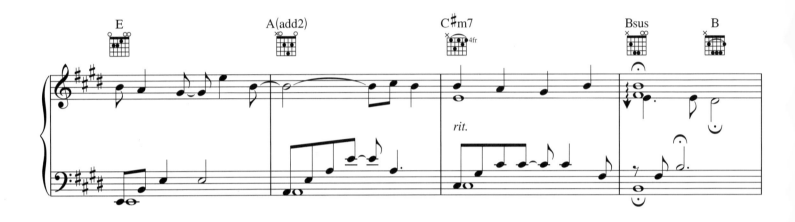

WHEN THE SUN GOES DOWN

Words and Music by
BRETT JAMES

sun goes _ down. _

54

ANYTHING BUT MINE

Words and Music by
SCOOTER CARUSOE

mine. *(Vocal 1st time only)*

Optional Ending

Repeat and Fade

BE AS YOU ARE

Words and Music by KENNY CHESNEY
and DEAN DILLON

Recorded a half step lower.

I GO BACK

Words and Music by
KENNY CHESNEY

NO SHOES NO SHIRT
(No Problems)

Words and Music by
CASEY BEATHARD

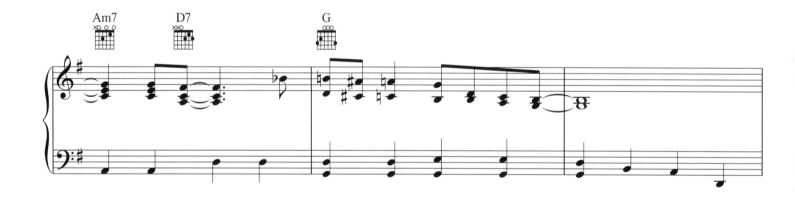

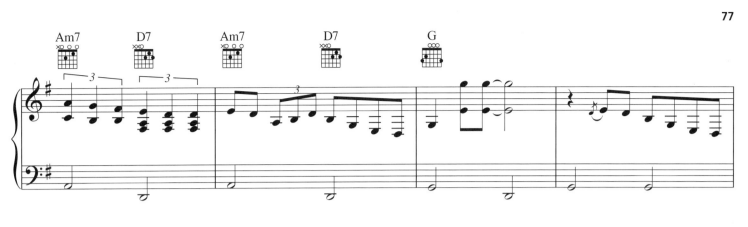

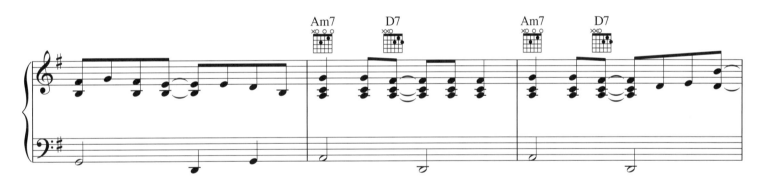

I've been up ____ to my neck ___ work-in' six ___
____ on a chair ___ and the sand ___

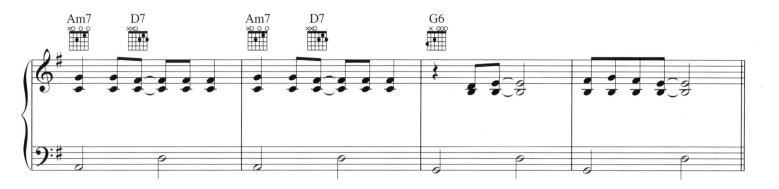

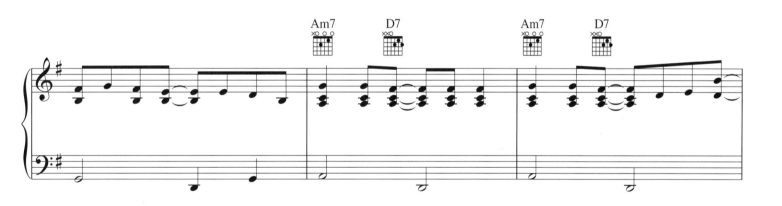

THE GOOD STUFF

Words and Music by CRAIG WISEMAN
and JIM COLLINS

NEVER WANTED NOTHIN' MORE

Words and Music by CHRIS STAPLETON
and RONNIE BOWMAN

I'M ALIVE

Words and Music by KENNY CHESNEY,
DEAN DILLON and MARK TAMBURINO

Lyrics: So damn eas- -y to say ___ that life's __ so hard. ___

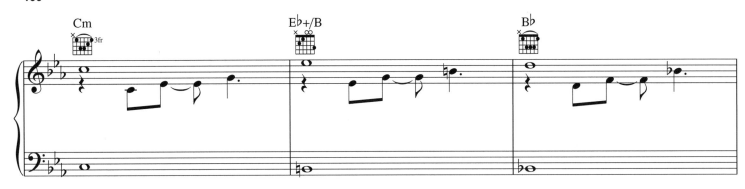

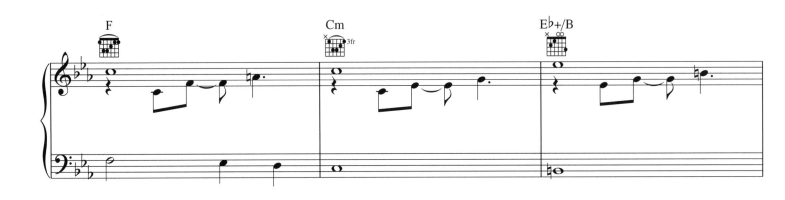

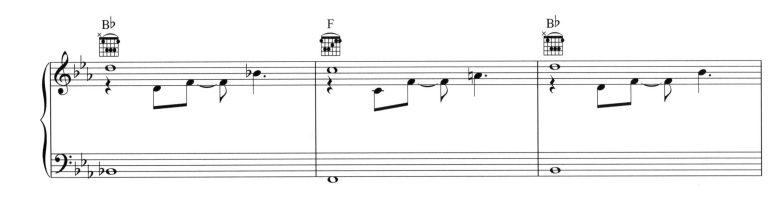

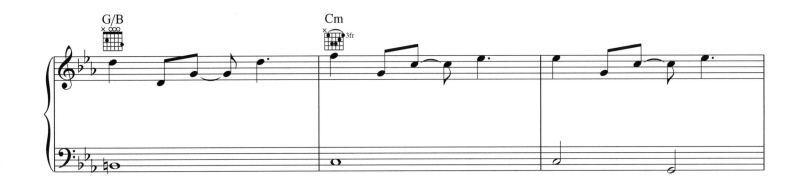

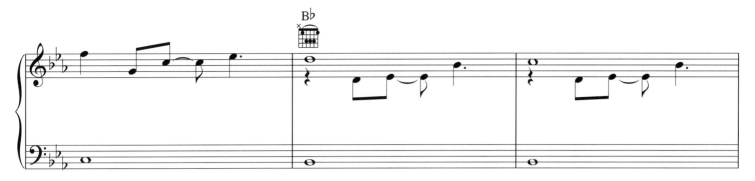

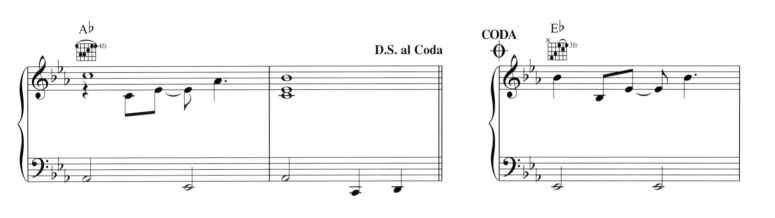

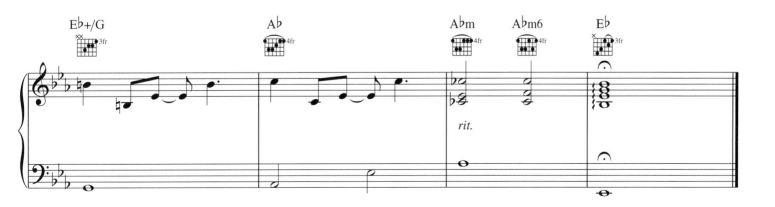